W9-AYQ-920

X-MOVES

Mighty MotoXers

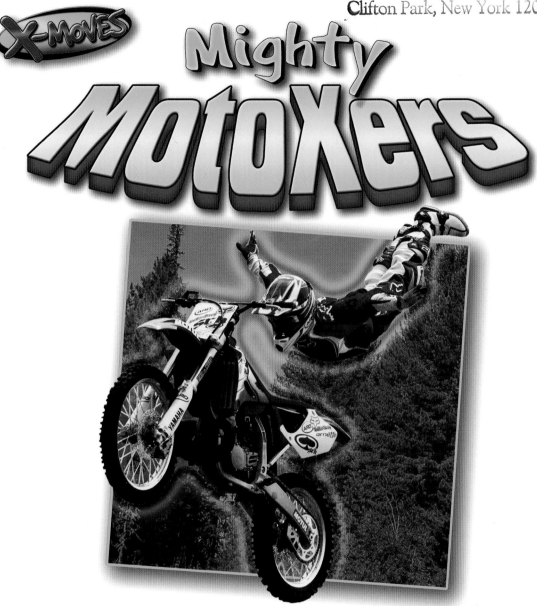

by Michael Sandler

Consultant: Basem Wasef
Motorcycle Expert and Author of *Legendary Motorcycles*

BEARPORT PUBLISHING

New York, New York

Credits

Cover and Title Page, © Mark Ralston/AFP/Getty Images; TOC, © Andreas Gradin/Shutterstock; 4, © Ryan Mahoney/PhotoCross; 5, © Paul J. Sutton/Duomo/Corbis; 6, © Ullstein Bild/The Granger Collection, NY; 7, © Stephen Wilson/World Picture News; 8, © Philipe Ancheta/Shutterstock; 9, © Julia Hoyle/PA Wire; 10, © Simon Cudby/Redbull Photofiles; 11, © Simon Cudby/Redbull Photofiles; 12, © Vaughn Youtz/Zuma Press; 13, © Tony Donaldson/Icon SMI; 14, © Icon SMI; 15T, © Bo Bridges/Corbis; 15B, © AP Images/Reed Saxon; 16, © Bo Bridges/Corbis; 17, © Vaughn Youtz/Zuma Press; 18, © Cliff Welch/Icon SMI; 19, © AP Images/Denis Poroy; 20, © ZSports/Zuma Press/Icon SMI; 21T, © Jeff Crow/Sport the Library/Icon SMI; 21B, © epa/Corbis; 22, © Dmitry Yashkin/Shutterstock.

Publisher: Kenn Goin
Senior Editor: Lisa Wiseman
Creative Director: Spencer Brinker
Photo Researcher: Daniella Nilva

Helmets are a motorcycle rider's most important piece of safety gear. If you try motorcross racing or freestyle, wear one. It's the only way to ride.

Library of Congress Cataloging-in-Publication Data

Sandler, Michael, 1965-
  Mighty motoXers / by Michael Sandler.
      p. cm. — (X-moves)
  Includes bibliographical references and index.
  ISBN-13: 978-1-59716-951-6 (library binding)
  ISBN-10: 1-59716-951-X (library binding)
  1. Motocross—Juvenile literature. 2. ESPN X-Games—Juvenile literature. I. Title.
  GV1060.12.S36 2010
  796.7'56—dc22

                              2009014616

For more information, write to Bearport Publishing Company, Inc., 101 Fifth Avenue, Suite 6R, New York, New York 10003. Printed in the United States of America.

10 9 8 7 6 5 4 3 2 1

Contents

Something Wild

Superstar Travis Pastrana had already made an almost perfect **run**. The judges gave him 99 out of 100 possible points. No one could beat the talented 15-year-old rider now. The first **X Games** gold in **freestyle** motocross was his.

Still, Travis had one run left. What trick should he do? *Why not something wild?* Travis thought. He **revved** his engine and roared across the dirt. Then he sailed off a ramp—in the wrong direction! Just for fun, Travis had jumped his bike off the course and straight into the cold waters of San Francisco Bay!

Travis Pastrana before a race

Travis's "Lazy Boy" trick helped him win the gold at the 1999 X Games.

Though Travis was just 15 years old at the X Games in 1999, he'd been riding for years. He got his first motorcycle when he was just four years old.

The History of Motocross

Before Travis was doing tricks, he was a motocross racer. Motocross is short for *motorcycle cross-country*. In motocross competitions, riders race lightweight **off-road** motorcycles on dirt tracks. They leap over hills and speed around sharp turns.

The sport grew out of motorcycle races held in England in the 1920s called scrambles. These races were made up of long rides over hills and through swamps. They grew very popular throughout Europe.

Soon the French shortened the courses and added man-made jumps. These new-style races spread quickly through Europe after World War II (1939–1945). By the mid-1960s, the sport started to become popular in the United States.

A rider during a scramble in 1928

6

World champion Stefan Everts racing in 2005

Belgian Stefan Everts is considered the greatest European motocross champion ever. He retired in 2006 after winning a record ten world titles.

American Motocross Racing

Today, top American racers compete in the **AMA** Motocross Championships, a series of 12 races held at different tracks around the country. Each of these events has two rounds, called motos. Riders receive points for each moto based on the order in which they finish. The rider with the best score after both motos is the overall winner.

Before retiring in 2007, Ricky Carmichael won more AMA races than any rider in history, 144 in all. His **successor** as top rider is James "Bubba" Stewart. James finished in 2008 with a perfect season. He won each of the 24 motos he competed in.

In 2007, Ricky Carmichael retired from motocross to try car racing. He and James Stewart are the only two riders to have ever achieved perfect AMA motocross seasons.

Motocross courses are one mile to one mile and a half (1.6 to 2.4 km) long. In most motos, riders race around a course for 30 minutes. After the 30 minutes are up, the riders race for two more full laps. The first rider to cross the finish line is the winner.

James Stewart (in front), was the champion of AMA's 2008 series.

Women's Motocross Racing

Motocross racing isn't only for men. Ashley Fiolek is the sport's top female racer. In 2008, she won the women's championship in her very first season. Amazingly, Ashley was only 17 years old.

Ashley's early success isn't the only thing that sets her apart. Ashley was born deaf. Unlike most riders, she can't hear the sound of her bike's revving engine to tell her when to change gears. Instead, she feels the engine's vibrations in her hands and body. These vibrations let her know when it's time to shift gears.

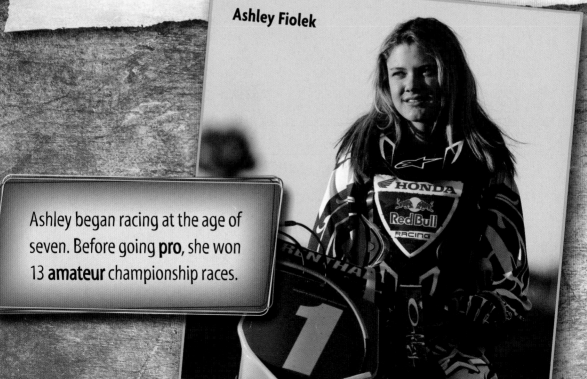

Ashley Fiolek

Ashley began racing at the age of seven. Before going **pro**, she won 13 **amateur** championship races.

Ashley Fiolek during a race in 2009

Freestyle Motocross

Motocross racing has always been **acrobatic**. During the jumps, riders fly through the air. So performing tricks in the air was a natural next step. Riders who fell behind in a race often tried them just for fun. Winners celebrated with special victory jumps.

In the 1990s, some riders got rid of the racing part altogether to focus on these tricks. A new type of motocross was born—freestyle!

Ex-racers Brian Deegan and Mike Metzger led the way, riding around the California desert, perfecting wild moves. Other riders saw videos of the pair and were encouraged to give it a try. Soon, freestylers were holding contests to show off their best tricks.

Brian Deegan performs a trick during a motocross event.

Mike Metzger kicks off the X Games in 2003 by jumping over the monorail at Disney's California Adventure Park.

For years, the backflip was the trick freestylers longed to do. They had seen it done on BMX bikes and wondered if it could be done on a motorcycle. In 2000, Carey Hart proved it could. Then, in 2002, Mike Metzger took it further, becoming the first to do back-to-back backflips in a freestyle run.

The X Games

The X Games is the biggest event in freestyle motocross, and Travis Pastrana is the Games' biggest star. Since his famous jump into San Francisco Bay in 1999, he's **dominated** the competition, winning the Freestyle gold medal five times. In 2006, he won Best Trick with a death-defying double backflip.

The only rider who can match a Travis Pastrana trick is Kyle Loza. He won gold medals in 2007 and 2008 for the Best Trick event.

In 2007, Kyle landed The Volt, a flying midair body spin. Then in 2008, he won with the Electric Doom. For this trick, Kyle jumped off his bike after flying off the ramp. Then he spun around wildly, kicking his legs. Finally, he jumped right back on his bike for the landing.

Travis's double backflip was the first ever in freestyle competition.

Kyle Loza

Kyle performing during the Best Trick event at the 2007 X Games

The X Games Freestyle motocross competition includes two events, Freestyle and Best Trick. In Freestyle, riders do a series of tricks on a jump-filled course. In Best Trick, riders do a single trick in the air after zooming up a ramp. In both events, judges score riders for both style and difficulty.

More Competitions

The X Games isn't the only freestyle motocross competition. Top riders also compete in events like the AST Dew Tour and the LG World Championships of Freestyle Motocross.

Nate Adams, known as the "King of the Backflip," won the Dew Tour three times. He also took four LG World Championships in a row. Then, in 2007, Nate was pushed from the top by Jeremy "Twitch" Stenberg. Jeremy stole Nate's crown by displaying a stunning variety of **whips** and backflips. Proving he was no fluke, Jeremy repeated as LG champion in 2008.

A step-by-step look at Nate Adams's backflip

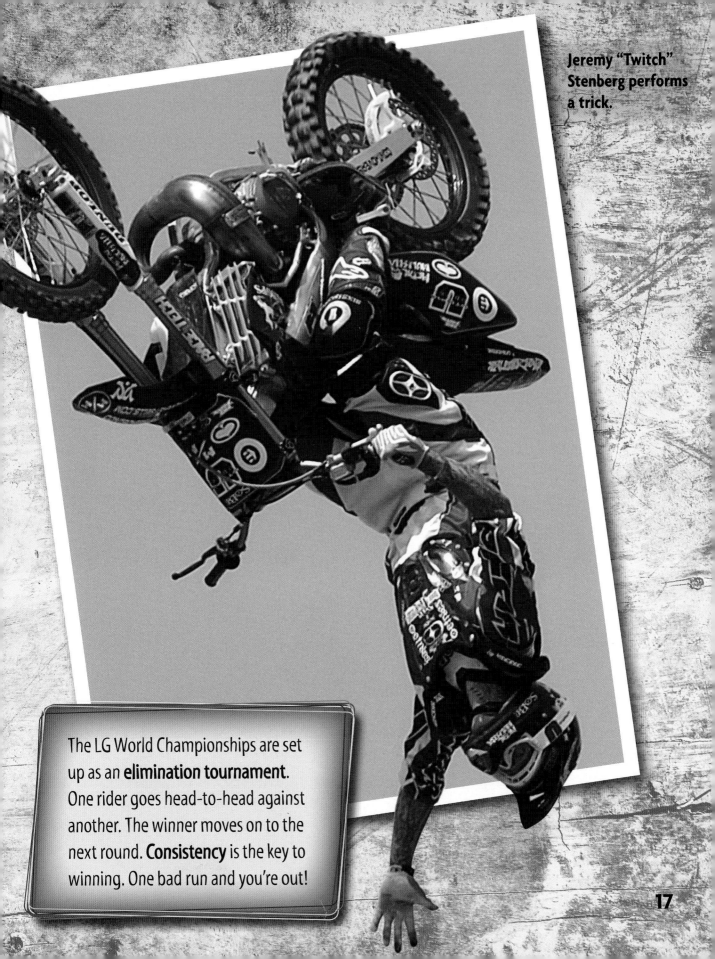

Jeremy "Twitch" Stenberg performs a trick.

The LG World Championships are set up as an **elimination tournament**. One rider goes head-to-head against another. The winner moves on to the next round. **Consistency** is the key to winning. One bad run and you're out!

Risky Business

Motocross's furious races and crazy tricks can be dangerous. Sprains, **concussions**, and broken bones are common. Travis Pastrana has had more than a dozen **surgeries**.

Riders try to be careful, but even the best make mistakes. Jeremy Lusk took Freestyle gold at the 2008 X Games and was named the year's top rider by *Transworld Motocross* magazine. Then, in February 2009, he crashed while trying a move called the Hart Attack—a tricky one-handed backflip. Jeremy failed to complete the spin and fell 20 feet (6 m) to the ground. Sadly, he died three days later.

Jeremy Lusk in 2008

Freestyle motocross rider
Todd Potter does a spin into
a foam pit during a practice.

How do riders safely learn new tricks?
They practice them hundreds of times
above foam pits before trying them out on
dirt. The pits are filled with foam blocks
that soak up the impact of a rider's fall.

Flying Higher

Motocross is constantly changing. In racing, new types of competitions are always **emerging**. Supercross, for example, took motocross from outdoor tracks into baseball and football stadiums. Now there is even arenacross—motocross races that can fit inside smaller indoor arenas.

Freestyle also changes, as riders push the limits of what's possible. Australian rider Robbie Maddison is pushing the hardest. Robbie is the world's greatest motorcycle distance jumper. In March 2008, he jumped a record-breaking 351 feet (107 m)!

Even other motocross daredevils think Robbie is **unique**. "Maddo is insane," says Travis Pastrana. He flies "a motorcycle farther than anyone ever dreamed."

James Stewart is not only a motocross champion. In 2009, he won the AMA Supercross Championship.

Robbie Maddison setting his world-record jump

A step-by-step look at Robbie's jump

Robbie made his world-record jump in Melbourne, Australia. How far is 351 feet (107 m)? It's almost exactly the length of a football field—including the **end zones**!

Motocross 101

To be the fastest racer and to perform the wildest tricks, motocross riders need the best gear and safety equipment.

Goggles
Protect your eyes from dirt and rocks; sometimes they are built into the helmet

Helmet
Keeps your head safe if you fall during a race or trick; always wear one

Gloves
Keep your hands protected and help you grip the handlebars

Body Armor
Plastic-covered foam that protects your body in crashes

Clutch
A lever you pull while changing gears

Engine
Bigger engines provide more power

Motocross Boots
Stiff and thick with steel toes

Glossary

acrobatic (*ak*-ruh-BAT-ik) using great skill and agility

AMA (AY-EM-AY) the American Motorcyclist Association; this group governs motocross racing

amateur (AM-uh-chur) an athlete who does not receive money for competing; an athlete who is not a professional

concussions (kuhn-KUSH-uhnz) temporary brain injuries caused by heavy blows to the head

consistency (kuhn-SISS-tuhn-see) the ability to repeat a task with the same level of skill

dominated (DOM-uh-*nayt*-id) did much better than, overwhelmed

elimination tournament (uh-*lim-uh*-NAY-shuhn TUR-nuh-muhnt) a sports event made up of a series of rounds with some competitors being eliminated after each round

emerging (i-MURJ-ing) appearing or developing

end zones (END ZOHNZ) the areas at either end of a football field where touchdowns are scored

freestyle (FREE-stile) a type of motocross riding in which the goal is to do the coolest tricks

off-road (AWF-rohd) meant for riding on unpaved terrain and not on regular roads

pro (PROH) professional; an athlete who gets paid to play a sport

revved (REVD) ran an engine at an increasing speed

run (RUHN) a single ride through a freestyle motocross course

successor (suhk-SESS-ur) a person who takes over a role from another person

surgeries (SUR-jer-eez) medical operations

unique (yoo-NEEK) one of a kind; like no other

whips (WIPS) tricks in which the rider whips the back of the bike sideways in the air

X Games (EKS GAMEZ) an extreme sports competition held every year

Bibliography

Dean, Josh. "The New Daredevil." *Rolling Stone* (August 7, 2008).

Pastrana, Travis, and Alyssa Roenigk. *The Big Jump: The Tao of Travis Pastrana.* New York: ESPN (2007).

Woods, Bob. *Motocross History.* New York: Crabtree Publishing (2008).

The New York Times

ESPN.com

Read More

Higgins, Matt. *The Insider's Guide to Action Sports.* New York: Scholastic (2006).

Johnson, Ben. *Motocross.* New York: Crabtree (2008).

Savage, Jeff. *James Stewart.* Minneapolis, MN: Lerner (2008).

Schaefer, A.R. *Extreme Freestyle Motocross Moves.* Mankato, MN: Capstone (2003).

Learn More Online

To learn more about motocross tricks, stars, and races, visit
www.bearportpublishing.com/X-Moves

Index